Why it is Easy to Control People when they are Afraid-Same in Private Life as in Politics-Trump's Motivation of Power and his Admiration of Putin

By:

Viora Mayobo

I dedicate this book (Why it is Easy to Control People when they are Afraid-Same in Private Life as in Politics-Trump's Motivation of Power and his Admiration of Putin?) to people across the globe, who willfully have avoided saying something or even speak out against bad policy, exhibited by many countries in almost every corner of earth. Everything that affects Mankind negatively, in every aspect of life today, is indicative of bad policy. And it is your responsibility as world citizens to do whatever you can to help create an atmosphere that's good for you, your children and your grandchildren, today and years to come. Please understand that everything this world is today has to do with what our great-great grandfathers did and did not find necessary to erect…

It therefore is important to understand fear and safety do not serve the same purpose: fear is there to intimidate, terrorize and impose, whereas safety has everything to do with safe-keeping, protecting, and shielding your interests against impositions.

Contents

Introduction

Life is full of give and take moments that sometimes leave you feeling hopeless. It is within your power to exercise good judgment to help retain your rights. The decision you make when in fear will determine where you end up in life – with a failed status or a successful one. Be quiet no more if things are not working out for you; be quiet no more if the political atmosphere isn't one that is built to benefit you, fully. Life shouldn't be intimidating, but rather a bit more enjoyable…

Why it is easy to Control People when they are Afraid, Same in Private Life as in Politics-Trump's Motivation of Power and his Admiration of Putin

I begin first by classifying what fear is not-
Fear is not a shield or a form of protection - erected to keep you from harm - and therefore cannot be used as a cover to shield yourself from in-coming. Because every time you try to protect yourself by seeking refuge in a shield of fear, you foolishly end up exposing every part of you that must be protected, you expose a hidden you…you're trying inadvertently to hide for safe-keeping, in the first place.
And is-
Fear works pretty much like a traitor who pretends to love and care deeply of your being while also working to expose your weaknesses. Shielding yourself in a wrap of fear makes you vulnerable in many ways than not…You unintentionally blow away your own cover and expose yourself to the enemy.

Fear and safety are two contrasting forces, flowing opposite of the other, with each catering to a different segment – terror, and safety.

It comes therefore as no surprise to some of us who have found ourselves hold up under the control of another being, for years, afraid, more than once. There were times, many times I did not feel prone to think or even know what was happening.

Knowing of what belie ahead gives you leverage over certain things in life – impositions, intimidation, abuse, etc., - as opposed to not. Out of fear, people, at least most, make decisions they know are wrong to begin with, but decide to give in and go with the flow, as that is the easy way out.

What most people don't seem to understand is that what we think is the easy way out...isn't always what it appears to be; it does in a reasonable number of times turn out to be the most deceiving notions and a misplaced conscious, decisions many have come to regret later in life.

When I left Zambia, I left small children with my brother, who is not hear with us today; a few months after leaving, my brother succumb to death. He had been sick a long while.

I had been dreaming when that call came in around midnight. In that dream, mother, my brother and I were trying to cross a river filled with green, slippery stuff. As mother and I were having such a hard time getting across, my brother seemed to be having fun; he stepped on one rock and then another and another. And just like that...he had made it across the river.

Instead of focusing on getting across, I took my time to admire the glitter, and then the phone rang. That call came in at a time when I was completely distracted from why I went to the river in the first place, which was to go across.

Before I could pick up the phone I almost knew what was to expect – bad news. For a few days, I wasn't in a mood to do anything, which from my past experiences indicates bad news, in most cases, the loss of a loved one.

Picking up the phone became such a scare for I knew what was to come of it – bad news.

Tears dripped down my face before I even said hello. I just picked up the receiver and there it was. My sister broke the news; she told me that my brother had just passed. Immediately, I fell to the ground, rolling all over in agony, wailing as loud only as I could.

The fact that I was unable to attend his funeral, and be a part of final farewell, has made my brother's death a carry-on baggage - one I will toil with me through life…to the end of my days, and I should.

Although I did not have a status by which to associate, I should have made a decision to attend my beloved brother's funeral.

For sure…life is full of trials and tribulations, but sometimes…it is best, out of the goodness our hearts, to make decisions that will not end up haunting us long as we live, and I've made quite a few of them over the course of this life-cycle.

A painter finds pleasure in painting which no one but the painter is aware of, whereas in writing, one has to be compatible with world citizens to produce tangible results. It therefore is well to assume decisions we make in life are influenced mostly by that which we find solace in and not the consequence that follows thereafter.

Knowing now that my brother's farewell was a once in a lifetime, one event in a life-cycle, I should have found it within my bruised heart to attend the funeral regardless of my status, at the time. Decision-making is perhaps most difficult, one of the toughest to have to deal with. Yes, sometimes we panic; we hurt, thereby failing to make the best of decisions.

I left home in pursuit of life; but because I was so afraid of being in a foreign country for a long time, for the first time, I forgot what brought me here, in the first place – which was to take care of all of my responsibilities including the accommodation of emergencies.

I instead veered off my initial path and diverted onto another and then another. By now…I was so far off the tracks that it was almost impossible to get back and start over. Looking back, I wish I had stayed the course; perhaps things wouldn't be as bad as they turned out.

Many people make marriage appear as though the best thing to ever exist, but that isn't always so. And I don't think I'll ever look at it from a positive perspective because of what I had to forgo in the name of marriage.

I was so afraid that the control that…that man had over me appeared normal to me, even when almost everyone around me gave voice of concern.

By the time I came to realize what was done to me was abuse, I already had two boys whom I loved and cared deeply about, making it difficult for me to leave.

In attempts to save my marriage…I lost control over my own life and got lost in the clutter. Navigating your way through the clutter of the world to get to the truth is like trying to make yourself understand something that is not understandable.

You will lose your sanity before you will ever get to the truth, which will be of no use. There can be nothing you can do with truth if you are crazy, for right and wrong, good and bad, love and abuse, tender and aggression, and all else will look the same from an even compromised mind. I was too much absorbed in my own thoughts to give any immediate options a chance.

I believe, given the amount of torture I've had to endure in this life-cycle, that…I am perhaps the most long-suffering of human beings ever lived…or at least I think.

Now, am I crazy? I don't know, but I would want to believe I'm not. There's absolutely nothing wrong with me, I believe; I'm one of those who have had to weigh their options more than once – should I go or should I stay?

Life is full of give and take moments that leave you toothless, especially if you have to choose between two rivals - your marriage and the well-being of your children, both of which are equally important. It's near impossible to choose one over the other.

I honestly could not pick my job or my marriage over my children; while a job is a must have in order to care for your children adequately…I was still susceptible for weighing my options, carefully. Which is why I chose to keep both – my children and my job, and do away with the extra burden - my marriage?

The decision to simply walk away from my marriage of 11 years was a difficult one, as it did not come by easily - especially because two innocent souls had already been involved, yet making that determination was something I was required to do if were to regain control of my self-worth.

To be afraid is humiliating and frustrating; to do nothing of the state of affair makes you a fool, in that you are completely aware of the dangers of accepting the intolerable when your boundaries are being over-stepped, time and again, and yet you don't seem to know what action to take – one that would lead you towards freedom.

Aside from having to worry about whether or not it is the right choice to make, you are put in a position where you have to wonder of what others will think of you, also. And that makes decision-making a more complicated aspect of life.

When people are afraid their right to exercise judgment is impaired. The what-if questions in that kind of environment take center-stage, while ignoring the rest – the whys, the when, the how…making the entire topic of fear all the more confusing.

It's not until you begin to look at a given circumstance from an inward perspective will you only then realize fear did in fact cloud your judgment in more ways than you thought possible. The same is true of life on political grounds. "The devil you know" mechanism swings into full action.

People in the modern world find it quite easy to place their bets on familiar territory more comfortably than they otherwise would on foreign grounds, even when their pocket book transactions are not any closer to being acceptable.

It sometimes makes a whole lot of sense to take a leap of faith if certain things aren't perceived as admissible to your inner self. Fear can be more powerful when justifiable than many people seem to understand.

Another fact that puts you in a somewhat similar position is money. It is near impossible to make sound decisions if the undercurrent of the prime driver of any given situation is money.

Money being the medium of exchange determines where an individual belongs; if you are with fewer numbers or with none at all, you undoubtedly make yourself assume you are poor. And when that is the case with you…don't suppose your mind is frail, as that is only human.

We as humans are more comfortable with our place in life, even if that means you earn close to nothing to be able to live comfortably. Something out of convenience I call 'fear of the unknown'. Human beings are more frightened when interacting with perplexing incidents than they are when dealing with circumstances of familiarity.

It is along those very lines do we find ourselves time and again swinging from side to side on a rocking ball. Swing baby swing till you no longer can swing.

The fact is…it is best to exhaust all the options available to you before you can decide to rest. You would have to understand the underlying concept of success to know that most those that make it in dear life are the ones willing to risk, even if that risk comes with a considerable price to pay, as that is the case in most instances that involve a great deal of change.

You get it right you break the cycle of struggle; you get it wrong you lose everything.

But that does not mean you rest easy; keep trying till you get it right. And I know that…that sounds like a surmountable challenge, like climbing a Mount Kilimanjaro, a tall mountain without proper hiking gear, just because it is.

Fear is the tallest mountain known to Mankind, and until you can figure out how to approach that mountain from different angles to make it appear less intimidating from your perspective, you will most likely spend your entire life relying on low laying fruit, which in most cases is already been salvaged and not good for human consumption.

And I say that from a heart of reason; that road – the road of fear - is one I've traveled more than once, and achieved different results, each time.

You just have to know your positioning – are you further away from the start of points and closer to the finish line? Or is that question in reverse order? The reason I ask is because it would be easier to go forward if the start point is much further, and the finish line much closer.

Politicians have come to realize that it is very easy to control people when they are afraid and powerless, than is it to control them when they are brave and rich.

When a person is afraid and poor he spends much of his time wandering around as though a lost soul, than thinking hard about what it is that must be done next to change the aftereffect. Which explains why majority of people who are afraid and poor are more inclined to make more mistakes in life, because their standing is one that comes from a compromised attitude?

A compromised altitude makes afraid and poor people more vulnerable to most other situations – in marriage, at work, in a country, etc., as that is a situation they can tolerate more comfortably.

Making a determination from a compromised posture does not necessarily make you foolish, it only makes you weak and hopeless, tolerating it does. It is there that you must be willing to take a leap of faith, to break the cycle of struggle, the cycle of fear and intimidation, the cycle of poverty, and retain your dignity.

Although that may be easily said than done, it is that same stance that will distinguish you from the rest. While almost everyone is busy contemplating whether or not to go forward, you will be busy trying to make those mountains a bit more comfortable to you. Freedom is not free, it is earned…

Most of us will most likely find ourselves climbing one mountain after another, just because we are eager to see what lies beyond every mountain in our life.

Some people would call that inquisitive, while others would characterize that as courage.

See, people are individuals, and what that means is that they draw conclusions of every situation from a different perspective; they look at things differently and from a different position.

Your positioning plays a major role in how you look at something; if your positioning is one that is dull, your view of things will be dull, also. Those with a better positioning will have a better view, and that gives them leverage over certain situations, because they will have the opportunity to analyze their view of things, better.

Many things that separate Mankind has everything to do with the leverage we have on circumstances, and that is true in private life as it is in politics.

When I listen to the lewd comments made by Donald Trump about his view of women, and his bully-pulpit positions, afforded to him and many others like him, by the nature of uneven grounds upon which we stand, I don't see how I can be exempt from having to voice my concerns.

If, for some reason, those remarks were made by Putin, the president of Russia, one viewed by some as the most influential and the most hated, at once, would that make it an okay thing to say? I don't think so, not in my wildest imagination would those comments be acceptable to me.

Those comments should not have come from any person or leader, let alone from someone running to be president of America. They are as demeaning and ugly as it will ever get. And they call to question our very democracy, here in America...

And yet we see members of the GOP, one of the major political parties in America, the most civilized country there's ever been in the history of Mankind, dancing around it...in cycles, supporting the candidate whose comments are so insidious and hard to fathom, for their own political gain, is really unimaginable and hard to dissect.

They seek very aggressively the vote of the minority, the poor, the same people they are working tirelessly to deny the right to vote, access to quality health care, equal pay for equal work, equal opportunity, better pay, good jobs, equality, leveled grounds upon which to compete - fairly, etc.

They indulge themselves in discrimination and fear tactics of the bygones while also presenting themselves as the change party; it is fair to say...they are not the solution but rather the problem making this world descent into the dark past.

We live in a society too full of fear and self-pity, thereby putting ourselves in compromised positions, no leverage. Negotiating for something without leverage makes you weak, and gives the other person more power and control.

It is for reasons mentioned above broken world systems have power and control over us (world citizens), because they are in charge of health care, education, housing, money, and everything that makes life…life, to begin with.

The beautiful necessity is when governments feel compelled to act irresponsibly without being held accountable for their impulsive behavior.

Normal people don't find it necessary to fix something they think is not broken. Mankind believes something can only be fixed if it's broken, but fixing what is broken isn't the only reason to want to work on something, perfecting requires fixing, too.

The same is true of knowledge; if people think they know when they don't, it's near impossible to bring them to the need, the need of wanting to know more.

There are very few people in this world who try to make something better if they think it's the best it can be, without realizing Mankind, being an individual, draws his perspective from a different angle. What he thinks is the best it can be, others aim to make perfect.

Knowing partial truth, and not the whole truth, puts you a weak position, same as that of an illiterate person. Partial truth is not a position; it holds no solid foundation to make your ground balanced. It's the whole truth or…nothing.

For example: suppose you walk into a store to buy a book that costs $6.00, but you only have $3.00, will you be able to buy that book? Or are you going to wait until you have the whole amount - $6.00?

Unless you are a fool, you would wait until you have the $6.00 in full before you can decide to go back to the store to purchase the book.

Making yourself appear pathetic by showing the entire world that you are needy…puts you in a compromising position; instead of being genuinely sympathetic to your situation, predators will use that to prey on you. This is something we have seen happen, time and again.

People with predatory behavior know when to respond to their instincts; they know how to spot their prey when they see it. It is for that same reason we teach our children not to develop tendencies of asking around.

Asking, even from people you know, was a normal practice in the times past, not anymore. A good neighbor will go out his way to ask if in fact you need help, but from what life has taught us, it is best to usually say, no, thank you.

It is near impossible to know who among us is genuine and who is offering fake help. Which is why it is good practice to teach our children to simply say no to offers originating from someone they think is kind.

Kindness is a hollow word in our society of to-day, because it is used to lure and manipulate the most vulnerable among us – women and children.

It is and must be in the interest of every responsible mother, father, son, and daughter to teach their children discipline, and the consequences of our actions. Our children must learn from a tender age to respect people – women, men, boys, and girls regardless of their possessions or where they come.

Politicians have mastered the traits of a weak mind and have learned to use them to manipulate and corrupt the word system to their advantage.

In the simplest of terms, what we do or say when we think no one is watching or listening, describes who we truly are as human beings. It describes in more definite ways who we really are. Simple terminology is all it takes to figure that out, nothing complicated.

Yes, we are no longer in the ancient times; and yes, we are no longer in the medieval era. But what is true also is that we are 2,016 years from the beginning of time, and yet we are still having the same discussions people we call ancient used to have ages ago.   They fought for freedom, against gender bias, inequality, and most other things, most of which we shouldn't be talking about today, here in the modern world.

Money isn't supposed to be used as a tool to decipher Mankind, and yet, by all accounts, that is still the case today. Why? This is how the world operates; it favors some more than others, and modern man seems to be handling that quiet well. We have allowed this world to descend into the darkest of ages.

It is in my opinion disingenuous to call some countries the third world when we are not any better than them. Civilization allows for civil yet genuine disagreements. Mankind is not built to agree on everything, but at least we can disagree in a respectful way.

I for one have lived through abuse, domestic violence, and I know there are no laws to protect women and their children, more. The reason we are even having this discussion as of now is because Trump is one of very few privileged, fat cats of Wall Street, judged by a set of different rules, otherwise we wouldn't be talking about it; he was caught boasting of how he inappropriately grabbed women by their private parts without their consent, a criminal offense punishable by jail time.

There are many in our jail system today serving life sentences for offenses less than those of Donald, and that speaks to the kind of democracy to which we have been exposed.

Women everywhere are still victimized, here in 2016. I can't resist asking, why? Why are we having this conversation, still? What is the broken congress doing to protect women at work, at home, in business? Like you do your best to look great and feel good about yourself, instead you are made to feel as though naked, a humiliating experience I'm all too familiar with.

It perhaps is well to assume no race or country in the modern world has piqued more in terms of civilization than those little savages of South Africa - the Bushmen. Indeed, there can be no known reasons why that could not be so, for the personal appearance and the habits of these little yellow savages are just as of now as they were then, and the familiarity of modern man with these little people is not much greater than it was yesterday - in the beginning of the history of man.

Where does the little person we call Bushman dwell? What is there country of origin? These questions are not so easily answered, because in reality the Bushman is not supposed to belong in any one country, much less possess land any more than wild animals.

If those ridiculous, lewd comments were made by a little person, we wouldn't be having this discussion right now; he would be locked up behind bars. And when I say little person, here, I be referring to the poor Joe, not the Bushman.

There's a good reason why every responsible parent does not want his/her children to have access to social media and most other websites considered unsafe; they would have to be at least 18 before they be allowed to create a profile.

And yet, there we are! Restricting our children access to the news, once an inferior activity, because it's rated 'R', not suitable for minors. I enjoyed watching news with my boys, 10 and 13, not anymore. News is now for junkies. What is happening, really?

I wonder why people of today think they are better than those of ancient times, when those same people are the ones who fully understood the ramifications of human cloning; they were fully aware that letting cloning take root would allow for doubles to roam freely among us.

Trump's motivation of power and his admiration of Putin place him along the lines of the worst dictators this world has seen; he lurks for control and hungers for a hidden power, both of which align well with self-centered ambitions of a tyrant.

Donald is an empty man, keenly anxious and hungry to see the victory of his cause; he watches the successes of dictators such Putin and Jong-un with breathless interest, and does not seem concerned at all with their affiliations and theoretical assertions and ideological constructions of their incitement of power.

He either fails to understand fully the distinction between democracy and dictatorship, or he has a deeper perception of the two than most of us are aware of. It does call to question his insight on governing and his ambition for power.

Although we can agree to disagree respectfully, we have to wonder why some people think being authoritative is desirable while also fighting for a system of government that encompasses right to freedom.

On the one hand, a democracy does within itself offer checks and balances, while on another hand, a dictatorship forfeits and relinquishes those same freedoms and rights to voice concerns.

For sure, Putin and Jong-un indulge themselves in the necessary evil of illiteracy of their people...at the expense of democracy, freedom, and peace...It therefore is of necessity to educate those in need of knowledge and afford them the chance to understand the difference, completely.

Of course, we as a people do have genuine objections and different views of how things are done in

Washington these days, emulating tyranny, for sure, sets us in a backward gesture, many that came before us died trying to break loose of.

The custom which the modern day renews comes to modern man from the creators of the commonwealth, ancient men of strong religious conviction and hearts, faithful men who erected their bureaucratic fabric as a shrine in which the word of God was worshiped.

The one fundamental with far-reaching deeds, the necessity for learning and understanding the distinction between working and being worked, can be interpreted in many different ways, languages…dependent upon one's mental capacity and country of origin.

Working and being worked are two words with very different meaning; working means civilization, while being worked can only means one thing – degradation. All forms of physical labor are honorable, and idleness of all forms disgraceful.

It therefore has been necessary for Mankind to understand that all beings of different races that have stood upon their feet did so largely by carefully laying, in general, an economic foundation, which at present day is still being perfected to meet the demands of all…

If, in too many instances, one race: black, or white, or Hispanic, or Asian began developing from a wrong end, it was primarily because neither of them properly understood the underlying concept.

Moods and lessons of a human mind are topics in life people don't have a desire for. The blessed mood in which the responsibility of the burden of the mastery is lightened, the unintelligible world is pleased and energized.

This has always been the distinction between Mankind, when looking for moods and goals. There is a common hallucination that brings out in authors a genuine desire to write, which is entirely based on moods and a brief moment of inspiration that allows them to labor in their unusual way.

Genuine writers are supposed to craft their thought when they have a peculiar desire or feel like it for their writing to be interesting…As an author myself I write only when I have a burning desire or a rare fortitude for it…and at no other moment.

About the Author

Viora is one of those that have found themselves fighting to keep control over their lives more than once, a race many have died trying to win. It is for that same reason she came to master the traits of self-control, discipline and freedom, and began to understand the underlying concept of life on uneven grounds…

Within her limitations, Viora has learned to cultivate her way through world cutter to achieve her desired goals, which can be intimidating, as is the case with every opportunity this world affords.

She wrote her first book (The Number Game by Viora Mayobo) soon after leaving the homeless shelter (Family Housing) in Los Angeles, CA, in which she shares her experiences as a homeless mother, now available on Amazon. She has also written 12 Hour Work Days-Helicopter Parents by Viora Mayobo, in which she offers word of encouragement and her opinion of life on minimum wage grounds, and uneven opportunity; it's now available on Amazon. And many other e-books on Amazon and Smashwords! Please purchase your copy of these books to show your support!   Coming Soon:

Why I smuggled for a Living

-carrying as much Weight as my body could possibly handle-45 minutes through a dark and thick terrain-risking it all for money

www.viorasbooks.com